D1633334

Target

Get back on track 3

Edexcel GCSE (9–1)
English Language
Writing

Julie Hughes

Pearson

Contents

This workbook has been developed using the Pearson Progression Map and Scale for English.

To find out more about the Progression Scale for English and to see how it relates to indicative GCSE 9–1 grades go to www.pearsonschools.co.uk/ProgressionServices

Helping you to formulate grade predictions, apply interventions and track progress.

Any reference to indicative grades in the Pearson Target Workbooks and Pearson Progression Services is not to be used as an accurate indicator of how a student will be awarded a grade for their GCSE exams.

You have told us that mapping the Steps from the Pearson Progression Maps to indicative grades will make it simpler for you to accumulate the evidence to formulate your own grade predictions, apply any interventions and track student progress. We're really excited about this work and its potential for helping teachers and students. It is, however, important to understand that this mapping is for guidance only to support teachers' own predictions of progress and is not an accurate predictor of grades.

Our Pearson Progression Scale is criterion referenced. If a student can perform a task or demonstrate a skill, we say they are working at a certain Step according to the criteria. Teachers can mark assessments and issue results with reference to these criteria which do not depend on the wider cohort in any given year. For GCSE exams however, all Awarding Organisations set the grade boundaries with reference to the strength of the cohort in any given year. For more information about how this works please visit: https://qualifications.pearson.com/en/support/support-topics/results-certification/understanding-marks-and-grades.html/Teacher

The activities in this workbook have been developed to support students in attaining the 5th, 6th and 7th Steps in the Progression Scale, focusing on those barriers to progression identified in the Pearson Progression Scale.

5th Step	6th Step	7th Step
A number of ideas gathered and **shaped** before **writing** with occasional revision to vocabulary after writing. Paragraphing is appropriate with some inconsistency, **sentences** are increasingly varied though largely for meaning, and **vocabulary** is wider with some consideration of impact.	Ideas are gathered and **sequenced** with some sense of logical progression before **writing** and more attention is paid to revision of vocabulary choices after writing. Paragraphs are used to organise content, **sentences** show growing awareness of structure and some evidence of deliberate crafting, and **vocabulary** is developing and used with some precision.	Ideas are gathered, sequenced and appropriately **shaped** before **writing,** and vocabulary is consistently reviewed after writing. Paragraphing is secure, **sentences** suggest some deliberate crafting of length and clause structure, and **vocabulary** is increasingly chosen with care and sometimes to achieve specific effect.

Unit title and **skills boost**	Pearson Progression Scale: Barriers (difficulties students may encounter when working towards this step)	Assessment Objectives
Unit 1 Gathering ideas for imaginative writing **Skills boost 1** How do I gather ideas? **Skills boost 2** How do I use a story structure? **Skills boost 3** How do I add the ingredients of a good story?	• May be reluctant to experiment with different planning formats. (Step 5) • Genre or text conventions and reader-writer relationship established in opening are not maintained throughout the text. (Step 5) • Emphasis on action and events in narrative, rather than on setting… There may be too many different events, underdeveloped with narrative detail, in the belief that a lot of action makes a story 'exciting'. (Step 6)	Communicate clearly, effectively and imaginatively (AO5)
Unit 2 Gathering ideas for transactional writing **Skills boost 1** How do I plan for audience, purpose and format? **Skills boost 2** How do I gather key ideas? **Skills boost 3** How do I develop my ideas with interesting detail?	• May be reluctant to experiment with different planning formats. (Step 5) • Genre or text conventions and reader-writer relationship established in opening are not maintained throughout the text. (Step 5) • Features of form may be considered and used 'ad hoc' while writing and therefore inconsistently or ineffectually used. (Step 6) • May use limited range of planning formats or simplistic models e.g. 'for and against' columns; bullet points. (Step 6)	Communicate clearly, effectively and imaginatively (AO5)
Unit 3 Structuring and developing your ideas – imaginative writing **Skills boost 1** How do I end my story effectively? **Skills boost 2** How do I develop interesting characters? **Skills boost 3** How do I think of a good opening?	• Limited or inconsistent awareness of 'writing as a reader' i.e. the need to make deliberate design choices with reader firmly in mind. (Step 6) • May have limited understanding of concept of 'crafting' writing. (Step 7) • Openings generally successful but endings less so e.g. in narrative, not so much a resolution as a new development; in non-fiction, simply an echo of the start. (Step 7)	Explain, comment on and analyse how writers use language and structure to achieve effects and influence readers (AO2)
Unit 4 Structuring your ideas – transactional writing **Skills boost 1** How do I organise my ideas into a logical order? **Skills boost 2** How do I write an effective introduction? **Skills boost 3** How do I write an effective conclusion?	• Limited or inconsistent awareness of 'writing as a reader' i.e. the need to make deliberate design choices with the reader firmly in mind. (Step 6) • May have limited understanding of concept of 'crafting' writing. (Step 7) • Openings generally successful but endings less so e.g. in narrative, not so much a resolution as a new development; in non-fiction, simply an echo of the start. (Step 7)	Organise information and ideas (AO5)
Unit 5 Making your meaning clear – sentences **Skills boost 1** How do I start and end a sentence? **Skills boost 2** How do I join my ideas into longer sentences? **Skills boost 3** How do I use punctuation correctly?	• Understanding of subordinate clause can be limited to idea that 'it doesn't make sense on its own' or that it can be 'moved around' in a sentence so that knowledge of how to form different types of subordinate clauses is partial or confused. (Step 5) • Lack of understanding of different purposes of apostrophes and commas; may be unaware of grammatical rules or have misconceptions. (Step 5) • Assumption that varying sentences is a mark of good writing, irrespective of context and purpose. (Step 6) • Errors or omission may be due to inconsistent proofreading, or imprecise understanding of rules for use of, e.g. commas to demarcate clauses or possessive apostrophes. (Step 6)	Use sentence structure for clarity, purpose and effect (AO6)

Unit title and skills boost	Pearson Progression Scale: Barriers (difficulties students may encounter when working towards this step)	Assessment Objectives
Unit 6 Writing sentences to create impact **Skills boost 1** How do I open my sentences to create impact? **Skills boost 2** How do I structure my sentences to create impact? **Skills boost 3** How do I use short sentences to create impact?	• May be more focused on vocabulary choice as a means of 'improving writing' rather than sentence structure and, with a limited repertoire of sentence openings, tends to automatically select subject-verb starts. (Step 5) • Assumption that varying sentences is a mark of good writing, irrespective of context and purpose. (Step 6) • Understanding of how to create sentence variety still insecure. (Step 7)	Use sentence structure for clarity, purpose and effect (AO6)
Unit 7 Writing paragraphs to create impact **Skills boost 1** How do I start paragraphs? **Skills boost 2** How do I structure my paragraphs to make my meaning clear? **Skills boost 3** How do I structure my paragraphs to create impact?	• May consider paragraphing accuracy a less important textual feature than, for example, spelling and punctuation. (Step 5) • May hold assumptions that paragraphs should be of a certain length and splice paragraphs to achieve it. (Step 6)	Use a range of sentence structures for clarity, purpose and effect (AO6)
Unit 8 Making your meaning clear – choosing effective vocabulary **Skills boost 1** How do I choose the best words? **Skills boost 2** How do I link my ideas? **Skills boost 3** How do I use techniques to add impact?	• May have limited strategies for improving vocabulary in their writing e.g. 'adding more' adjectives and adverbs. (Step 5) • Likely to use a limited range of adverbials. (Step 5)	Use a range of vocabulary and sentence structures for clarity, purpose and effect (AO6)
Unit 9 Creating impact with vocabulary – imaginative writing **Skills boost 1** How do I choose words for effect? **Skills boost 2** How do I use language techniques to create images? **Skills boost 3** How do I review and improve my vocabulary choices?	• Over-reliance on familiar similes to create description e.g. 'he was as quick as lightning' or 'I felt as cold as ice'. (Step 6) • May be more concerned about ensuring clarity of ideas and conveying literal meanings than creating stylistic effects e.g. through figurative language. (Step 6)	Use a range of vocabulary and sentence structures for clarity, purpose and effect (AO6)

① Gathering ideas for imaginative writing

This unit will help you to come up with ideas for an imaginative writing task.
The skills you will build are to:

- find interesting ideas
- use a story structure to make your ideas exciting to read
- use the ingredients of a successful story.

In Paper 1 of the exam, you will be asked to tackle an imaginative writing task like the one below. This unit will help you to plan your response.

Exam-style question

Look at the images provided.

Write about a celebration.

Your response could be real or imagined.

You may wish to base your response on one of the images.

(40 marks)

The three key questions in the **skills boosts** will help you to gather ideas for your imaginative writing task.

1 How do I gather ideas?

2 How do I use a story structure?

3 How do I add the ingredients of a good story?

Look at three students' story plans on page 2. They were written in response to the task above.

Exam-style question

Write a story about a celebration.

Plan A
- Wake up on my birthday
- No presents on my bed
- No one downstairs
- Feel sad, sit and cry
- Friends rush in shouting 'surprise'
- Go out for celebration and feel really happy

Plan B
- Won lottery
- Spent days buying stuff and celebrating
- Bought mum a house
- Got abuse on social media
- Best friend avoids me
- Start feeling very lonely
- Meet new friend who doesn't know about money

Plan C
- Score winning goal for first team
- Get selected for local league side
- Celebrate with friends who were in crowd
- Play first game for local league side
- Get into bad tackle with other player who is a friend
- Other player has broken leg from tackle
- Get sent off and lose place in team
- Go out and see rest of team celebrating
- Friend won't speak to me
- Spend all my time practising
- Get selected for premier league side
- Score winning goal in cup final
- Celebrate with team
- Friend who broke leg is there but don't speak to him

① All of these plans could be improved. Match ✐ the comments with the plans.

Plan A ⦾   ⦾too many events mean nothing will be developed with interesting details

Plan B ⦾   ⦾no real ending to story

Plan C ⦾   ⦾story is dull and a bit predictable: no excitement for reader

② ⓐ Choose one of the plans and write ✐ **two or three** sentences about how it could be improved.

Plan A ☐   Plan B ☐   Plan C ☐

Improvements: ....

....

....

....

ⓑ This task will be judged by people of your own age. Which plan is **most suitable** for the audience? Explain ✐ your choice.

....

....

....

1 How do I gather ideas?

One way to gather ideas is to use thought association. This means identifying the key word or idea in the title and writing down everything it makes you think about. You can then choose the most exciting or interesting ideas and fit them into a story structure.

1. Look at these ideas that a student has thought of related to the idea of 'celebration'.
   Add two or three more of your own ideas.

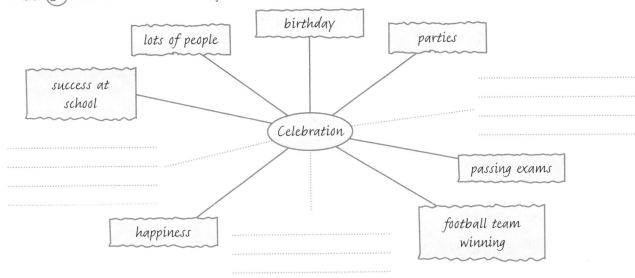

When you have chosen the most exciting ideas, one way to start planning is to ask yourself 'who', 'what' and 'where' questions. Look at how one student has used some ideas from question 1 above and made notes about the first image on page 1.

2. Now look at the second image on page 1. Use some of the ideas from question 1 above and then answer the 'who', 'what' and 'where' questions to gather ideas about characters, settings and events.

? What has happened?

....

....

....

? Who's there?

? Where are they?

Sticking to **two or three** characters means you can write about them in more detail.

....

2 How do I use a story structure?

When you have gathered some ideas, you should think about the structure of your story.

Look at this basic structure of an imaginative writing response.

Beginning – character and setting	Middle – the event or problem	End – the problem is resolved
Introduces the characters, their situation and the setting.	A problem or crisis happens and needs to be faced by the characters.	The characters deal with the problem. The story can end on a happy or a sad note.

For example, this is how one student has used an idea about celebration. Notice how extra story detail has been added to each stage.

I go to a football match with my dad and my sister Lucy. Stadium very big and very crowded. Team scores winning goal, crowd celebrate.	I get lost in crowd. Very frightened. Push through crowd trying to find Dad and Lucy. Announcement made on tannoy.	I am found by team's captain. He takes me to my dad. Then we all get to go and celebrate with team.

① It is a good idea to stick to one main event so that you can describe it in detail. Think again about the second image on page 1 and come up with ✏ **three** ideas for a main event.

  i. ....

  ii. ....

  iii. ....

② Your first ideas are not always your best ideas. Choose the most exciting or interesting idea from the three above and plan ✏ a story using the three-part structure.

Beginning	Middle	End

③ All three parts of your story should be of a similar length. Look again at your answer to question ② and see if there are any gaps in your plan.

• Your **beginning** should set the scene: is there enough detail about characters and setting?
• Your **ending** should be believable and not too sudden: how will your characters be feeling at this point?

4   Unit 1 Gathering ideas for imaginative writing

How do I add the ingredients of a good story?

When you have planned your story structure, it is a good idea to think about whether you have used the ingredients for a good story. These include:

• an engaging plot • interesting characters • some mystery or suspense • a satisfying ending.

Look at this student's plan for a story about a celebration.

Beginning

Woke up on birthday. Had party with friends. Parents gave me new bike. All my friends were jealous. Joined cycling club and raced every weekend. Stopped seeing friends. Entered big national race. Practised every day.

Middle

Race day comes. Wake up nervous. Have big breakfast and drive to race. Big shock on start line. Next to me is best friend. Best friend falls off bike during race. I race past him.

End

I win the race and get my medal. There is no one to celebrate with as all friends are at hospital with my best friend. I celebrate on my own.

1 This student has included too much action and readers might find it boring. Draw a line ✏ through any action you think is not necessary.

2 The best stories have some mystery or suspense.

   a Which of the following ideas would add more mystery or suspense to the story? Tick ✓ it.

     ☐ The narrator could find out after he has won that his best friend was in the race.

     ☐ The best friend could be injured in a crash with the narrator.

   b Add ✏ your own ideas to the plan above to achieve mystery or suspense.

3 Readers like to take sides in a story. It is a good idea to create a hero and a villain.

   a Outline ✏ how a character from the plan above could be made into a hero.

     ....

     ....

     ....

     ....

   b Briefly explain ✏ who could be the villain and how readers could be made to dislike him/her.

     ....

     ....

4 Readers like an ending where the hero wins and the villain is punished. Use your ideas for question 3 about characters to note ✏ down some details to make it either a sad or a happy ending.

....

....

....

Sample response

To plan a successful answer to an imaginative writing task, you need to:

- think carefully about the key ideas in the task
- ask 'who', 'what' and 'where' questions about the task
- use a three-part story structure
- think about creating heroes and villains, mystery and suspense and a developed ending.

Now look again at this exam-style writing task, which you saw at the start of the unit.

Exam-style question

Look at the images provided.

Write about a celebration.

Your response could be real or imagined.

You may wish to base your response on one of the images. **(40 marks)**

Look at one student's plan for the imaginative writing task.

(**1**) How could this plan be improved? Add 🖉 your ideas about heroes/villains and another detail that would add even more mystery or suspense to the story.

(**2**) How could the story end? Think about whether to add a happy or a sad ending. Note 🖉 your ideas in the plan.

> <u>Beginning</u>
> Home with friends on winter's night. Celebrating end of exams. Parents away. House is miles from anywhere.
>
>
> <u>Middle</u>
> Stranger comes to door. Hands over a parcel. Parcel has 'do not open' written on front. Best friend laughs – says we should open it.
>
>
> <u>End</u>

Your turn!

You are now going to **plan** your response to the exam-style task on page 1.

1 Think about 'who', 'what' and 'where'. Write 🖉 your ideas in the spaces below.

(?) Who?

(?) What? (What is your main event?)

(?) Where? (What is your main setting?)

2 Now fit your ideas into a three-part story structure. Make notes 🖉 below.

Beginning	Middle	End

3 Go back over your plan. Make sure you have thought about:

- heroes and villains
- mystery or suspense
- your ending – will it satisfy an audience?

Adjust 🖉 your plan if necessary.

Review your skills

Check up

Review your response to the exam-style question on page 1. Tick ✓ the column to show how well you think you have done each of the following.

	Not quite ✓	Nearly there ✓	Got it! ✓
gathered ideas	☐	☐	☐
used a story structure	☐	☐	☐
added the ingredients of a good story	☐	☐	☐

Look back over all of your work in this unit. Note ✏ down the **three** most important ingredients of a good story.

1. ....

2. ....

3. ....

Need more practice?

Plan your response to the exam-style question below.

Exam-style question

Write about a time when you, or someone you know, had to work hard at something.

Your response could be real or imagined.

(40 marks)

How confident do you feel about each of these **skills?** Colour ✏ in the bars.

1 How do I gather ideas?

2 How do I use a story structure?

3 How do I add the ingredients of a good story?

② Gathering ideas for transactional writing

This unit will help you to gather ideas for a transactional writing task. The skills you will build are to:

* gather ideas that suit audience, purpose and format
* come up with appropriate key ideas
* add interesting detail to develop key ideas.

In the exam, you will be asked to tackle a question like the ones below. This unit will prepare you to write a response to such questions.

EITHER:

Exam-style question

Write the text for a speech you will give to your peers exploring the idea that the internet is a dangerous tool.

In your speech, you could consider:
* the benefits of the internet
* the risks of using the internet
* things that people can do to stay safe online

as well as any other ideas you might have.

(40 marks)

OR:

Exam-style question

Write an article for a national newspaper about the benefits of modern technology for older people.

In your article, you could include:
* what types of technology are available
* how technology could make their lives easier
* where to get help with modern technology

as well as any other ideas you might have.

(40 marks)

The three key questions in the **skills boosts** will help you to gather ideas for when you are writing to present a viewpoint.

① **How do I plan for audience, purpose and format?**

② **How do I gather key ideas?**

③ **How do I develop my ideas with interesting detail?**

Exam-style question

Write the text for a speech you will give to your peers exploring the idea that the internet is a dangerous tool.

In your speech, you could consider:

• the benefits of the internet

• the risks of using the internet

• things that people can do to stay safe online

as well as any other ideas you might have.

(40 marks)

Look at how one student has planned for this task.

Can be addictive

Can be good for information/news – helpful for homework

Good for comparing insurance and fuel bills

Internet

Good for planning holidays

Good for online shopping – saves money without leaving home

Viruses can be downloaded by accident

Good for music and watching TV/films

(1) The student has included some ideas that are unsuitable for a young audience. Draw a line through them and add **two** ideas below that are more appropriate for a teenage audience.

i. ....

....

ii. ....

....

(2) The student has used only two of the bullet points from the question. Note down **two** ideas that could be used to answer the bullet point about safety online.

i. ....

....

ii. ....

....

(3) The student has added extra detail to only one of the main ideas. What interesting details could be added to the point about the internet being addictive? Write **two** ideas to develop this point.

i. ....

....

ii. ....

....

How do I plan for audience, purpose and format?

Before you begin to gather ideas, you need to make sure you are clear about the audience, purpose and format for the task. It is a good idea to underline words in the question that give you ideas about who you will need to write for (audience), why you are writing (purpose) and what form your answer should take (format).

Look at how one student has underlined key words in the first exam-style question on page 9.

Exam-style question

Write the text for a <u>speech</u> you will give to your <u>peers exploring</u> the idea that the internet is a dangerous tool.

In your speech, you could <u>consider</u>:

• the benefits of the internet

• the risks of using the internet

• <u>things that people can do</u> to stay safe online.

Notes about audience, purpose and format can then be made like this.

Format – speech – can be informal

Purpose – explore/consider means look at both sides; things that people can do means offer warnings/advice

Audience – peers means people my age (teenagers) so include things about music, films and social networking. Will need advice about giving out personal information.

(1) Underline (A) key words in the exam-style question below that give you ideas about the audience, purpose and format.

Exam-style question

Write an article for a national newspaper about the benefits of modern technology for older people.

In your article, you could include:

• what types of technology are available

• how technology could make their lives easier

• where to get help with modern technology.

(2) Now make notes about the audience, purpose and format. Think about:

• how formal your writing needs to be: do you know the audience?

• your point of view: do you need to write about both sides of the topic, or make your own opinion clear? Do you need to give advice?

• what information your audience will need.

....

....

....

....

....

2 How do I gather key ideas?

When you have thought about your audience, purpose and format, you will be able to gather ideas that are appropriate. A good place to start is by using the information provided with the task.

Look again at this writing task from the start of the unit. You are going to start to plan your response.

Exam-style question

Write an article for a national newspaper about the benefits of modern technology for older people.

In your article, you could include:

• what types of technology are available

• how technology could make their lives easier

• where to get help with modern technology

as well as any other ideas you might have.

One way to start planning is to use thought association. This means spending one minute writing down everything that comes into your head about the topic. You could use a spider diagram, or a list.

(1) Spend **one minute** adding ✐ more ideas to the spider diagram below.

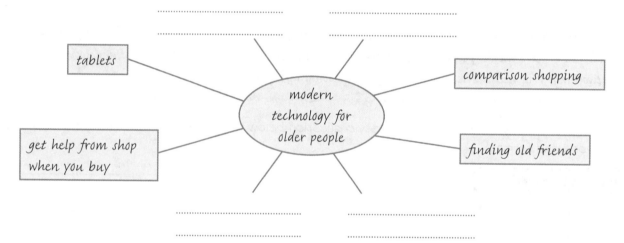

Now use the bullet points in the exam-style question to structure your plan. Look at one student's planning table below: there is one idea for each of the bullet points.

(2) Add ✐ your ideas from question (1) to the student's table.

Types of technology	Making life easier	Where to get help
tablet	comparison shopping	shop when you buy

③ How do I develop my ideas with interesting detail?

When you have gathered ideas that suit the audience, purpose and format of the task, you will need to develop them with interesting details. These will make your ideas seem more believable and trustworthy. Details can be:

- facts or statistics
- examples from your own experience.

You can make these up for the exam, but make them believable.

Look at one student's plan for the article about modern technology for older people.

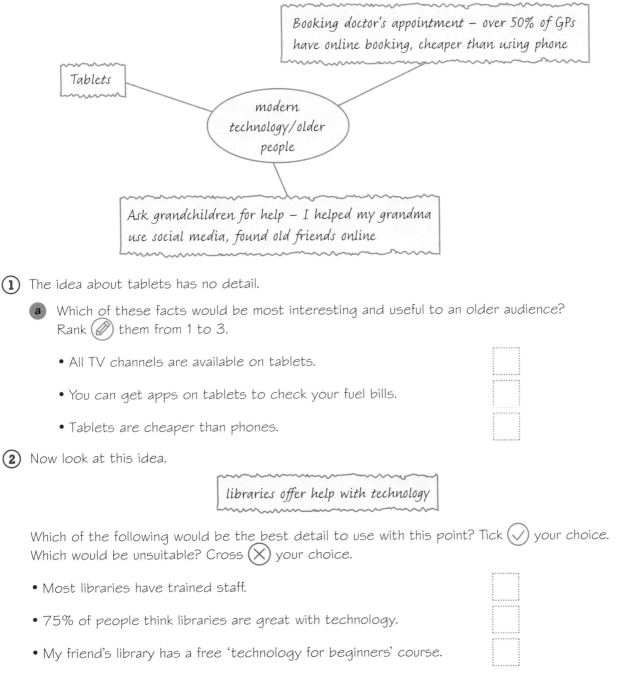

> Booking doctor's appointment – over 50% of GPs have online booking, cheaper than using phone

> Tablets

> modern technology/older people

> Ask grandchildren for help – I helped my grandma use social media, found old friends online

① The idea about tablets has no detail.

   a Which of these facts would be most interesting and useful to an older audience? Rank 🖉 them from 1 to 3.

- All TV channels are available on tablets.

- You can get apps on tablets to check your fuel bills.

- Tablets are cheaper than phones.

② Now look at this idea.

> libraries offer help with technology

Which of the following would be the best detail to use with this point? Tick ✓ your choice. Which would be unsuitable? Cross ✗ your choice.

- Most libraries have trained staff.

- 75% of people think libraries are great with technology.

- My friend's library has a free 'technology for beginners' course.

Sample response

To gather ideas for a transactional writing task, you should:

- think carefully about what will suit the audience, purpose and format
- use the bullet points in the task
- add details like facts, statistics and personal experience.

Now look again at the exam-style writing task from the start of the unit.

Exam-style question

Write an article for a national newspaper about the benefits of modern technology for older people.

You could include:

- what types of technology are available
- how technology could make their lives easier
- where to get help with modern technology

as well as any other ideas you might have.

(40 marks)

Look at another student's plan for this task.

modern technology/older people

- [ ] Many useful apps are free
- [ ] Phones
- [ ] Can have music on phone
- [ ] Tablets
- [ ] Get a 'how to' book from the library
- [ ] Phones mean you can get help in emergency
- [ ] Online shopping
- [ ] You can save 50% shopping online
- [ ] Libraries can help
- [ ] Find old friends
- [ ] Get help from shop
- [ ] My grandma found her best friend from school

(1) This student has a lot of ideas but has not structured the plan.

   (a) Label ✏ each idea with **what (w)**, **how (h)**, or **where (wh)**.

   (b) Cross ✗ through any ideas or details that do not suit the audience, purpose or format.

   (c) Add ✏ detail to make sure each of the ideas is developed in an interesting way.

Your turn!

You are now going to plan your response to this exam-style task.

Go back to page 11 to remind yourself of the format, purpose and audience for the task.

Exam-style question

Write the text for a speech you will give to your peers exploring the idea that the internet is a dangerous tool.

In your speech, you could consider:

• the benefits of the internet

• the risks of using the internet

• things that people can do to stay safe online

as well as any other ideas you might have.

(40 marks)

(1) Use thought association for **one minute** to gather ideas about the topic. Note ✏ them here.

internet
risks/benefits

(2) Now develop your best ideas with detail, and structure them using the bullet points in the writing task. Use this table to draft ✏ your plan.

Bullet points	Ideas	Detail
Benefits of internet		
Risks of internet		
How to stay safe online		

(3) Now think again about audience, purpose and format. Are all your ideas and details suitable? If not, replace ✏ them with more appropriate alternatives.

Review your skills

Check up

Review your response to the exam-style question on page 15. Tick ⊘ the column to show how well you think you have done each of the following.

	Not quite ⊘	Nearly there ⊘	Got it! ⊘
planned for audience, purpose and format	☐	☐	☐
gathered key ideas	☐	☐	☐
developed my ideas with interesting detail	☐	☐	☐

Look over all of your work in this unit. Note ✏️ down the **three** most important things to remember when gathering ideas for writing to present a point of view.

1. ....

2. ....

3. ....

Need more practice?

Plan your response to the exam-style question below.

Exam-style question

Write the text of a speech you will give to your peers, encouraging them to take up a healthy lifestyle.

In your speech, you could explain:

• why a healthy lifestyle is important

• why people find a healthy lifestyle difficult

• how to lead a healthy lifestyle

as well as any other ideas you might have.

(40 marks)

How confident do you feel about each of these **skills?** Colour ✏️ in the bars.

① How do I plan for audience, purpose and format? ☐☐☐☐

② How do I gather key ideas? ☐☐☐☐

③ How do I develop my ideas with interesting detail? ☐☐☐☐

③ Structuring and developing your ideas – imaginative writing

This unit will help you to structure and develop your ideas for the imaginative writing task. The skills you will build are to:

* plan a satisfactory ending

* develop your characters

* create an exciting opening.

In the exam, you will be asked to tackle a writing task like the one below. This unit will prepare you to write your own response to this question.

Exam-style question

Write about a time when you, or someone you know, told a lie.

Your response could be real or imagined.   (40 marks)

The three key questions in the **skills boosts** will help you to structure and develop your imaginative writing.

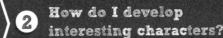

1 How do I end my story effectively?   **2** How do I develop interesting characters?   **3** How do I think of a good opening?

Look at one student's plan for the narrative writing task above on page 18.

Beginning	_Sat in classroom, very bored_
	Tom and I are playing with a football
	Teacher keeps telling us to put it away
Middle	_I kick football hard and it breaks the window_
	Teacher asks who did it
	I say Tom did it
	Tom gets excluded
End	_Tom refuses to see me_
	Tom spends all his time studying for exams at home
	I mess about at school

1 This student has used a good story structure and kept to two main characters.

a Think about the **beginning**: which opening would be most effective? Circle Ⓐ your choice.

> **?** A description of the football going through the window.

> **?** A description of the boys playing football.

> **?** A description of the teacher.

b Write 🖉 **one** sentence explaining your choice.

....

....

....

....

2 **a** Think about the **ending**: which ending would be most effective? Circle Ⓐ your choice.

> **?** Tom passes all his exams and goes to university. The narrator never sees him again.

> **?** The narrator meets Tom and apologises. Tom forgives him.

> **?** The narrator ends up unemployed while Tom goes to university and becomes a successful lawyer.

b Write 🖉 **one** sentence explaining your choice.

....

....

....

....

How do I end my story effectively?

Your ending should fully develop the main event. Good stories also show how the main event has affected the characters.

Look at this story plan one student drew up in response to the writing task at the start of the unit.

> Jane is going on her first skiing holiday with her family. On the plane, she meets a boy she likes. To impress him, she says she is an excellent skier. They arrange to ski together the following day.

> She meets the boy at the top of a difficult ski run. He looks very confident. Jane is so keen to impress him that she offers to go first down the slope. She stands at the top and gets ready to ski.

> Jane breaks her leg and the boy laughs. She never sees him again.

The ending is very brief and it does not develop either the main event or the characters. Using one of the following techniques would make it more satisfying for readers.

The lucky ending	Jane pretends to wait for other people to go first. Snow starts to fall and within minutes the slope is closed.
The surprise ending	Jane falls over within five metres. The boy follows and falls over near her. They turn and look at each other. They realise that neither can ski.
The ending that teaches the character a lesson	Jane breaks her leg in the fall and has to be airlifted to hospital. The boy overhears her telling the paramedics that she can't ski.

① Finish ⊘ each idea in a way that will satisfy the reader. Think about how the main event has affected the two characters.

② Which of the endings above would be most satisfying to a reader? Write ⊘ one sentence explaining your choice.

....

....

....

How do I develop interesting characters?

To make your narrative writing engaging all the way through, you need to create believable characters. One way to do this is to 'show' what they are like, rather than 'tell'.

Look at these two examples about the character Tom from the story about a lie on page 18.

> **A.** Tom loved football and played for the school team. Tom was really tall and great at headers.

> **B.** Tom's head nearly hit the classroom ceiling when he headed the ball. The ball sailed towards me over the desks. All the practice with the school team was worth it as everybody turned and clapped.

In the second example, it is the action that 'shows' rather than 'tells' the reader about Tom. This makes it easier for the reader to picture him and start to like him as a character.

① Stories need heroes and villains to make them exciting for a reader. Which of the following uses the 'show not tell' technique to make readers start to hate Tom? Tick ✓ your choice.

> **A.** The ball sailed towards me over the desk. All the practice with the school team paid off as it hit me hard between the eyes. Tom laughed.

> **B.** The ball sailed towards me over the desk. It hit me between the eyes. He played for the school team and hated me because I was no good at football.

② Try using this 'show not tell' technique to make the narrator into a more believable character.

> I was thin and small. I had never been any good at football. Nobody ever picked me to be on their team.

First, decide whether you want the reader to like or dislike your narrator. Then think about what action you could use to show the reader, rather than telling. You could think about:

• how the character moves (actions)

• what the character's body language is like

• how other people react to him.

Note down ✏ your ideas below.

Actions ....

....

....

Body language ....

....

....

How other people react ....

....

....

3 How do I think of a good opening?

Your imaginative writing will need to have an engaging opening so that readers want to read the whole story. One way to do this is to use a flashback technique, so that you interest your readers from the first sentence.

Look at these three openings to the story about a lie on page 18.

Create a mystery – this makes readers want to know what has happened.	Crash! The football sailed from my toe straight out of the window.
Start with conflict or danger – this will create tension from the very beginning.	I know I shouldn't have told the lie. I would regret it for the rest of my life. It was only a small lie at the time, but it caused so much trouble.
Start with action – this grabs the reader's attention as they will want to know more about what is happening.	I froze. The teacher looked up from her marking. Tom and I sat very still and tried to look invisible. My stomach churned with fear.

1 a Draw lines to match each technique to a story opening.

   b Which opening do you think is the **most** effective? Tick your choice.

   c Write **one** sentence explaining why you think readers would enjoy the style of opening you chose.

_____

_____

Notice that the three techniques above do not start with a boring explanation about the setting, such as:

> I was sitting in a classroom with Tom

A flashback can then be used to explain how the story began. Look at this example for the first opening.

> Crash! The football sailed from my toe straight out of the window. It had been a very boring French lesson until then.

2 Try finishing these lines for two more openings.

I know I shouldn't have told the lie. I would regret it for the rest of my life. It was only a small lie at the time, but it caused so much trouble. We had been sitting in a boring French lesson	I froze. The teacher looked up from her marking. Tom and I sat very still and tried to look invisible. My stomach churned with fear. I meant to pass the ball back to Tom but

Sample response

To structure your imaginative writing, you need to think about:

- developing your main event into a satisfying ending
- creating believable characters by showing, not telling
- starting with action, mystery or conflict to engage your readers from the very first sentence.

Look again at the imaginative writing task from the exam-style question at the start of the unit.

Exam-style question

Write about a time when you, or someone you know, told a lie.

Your response could be real or imagined.

(40 marks)

(**1**) Now look at one student's plan for this question.

To try to impress a new rich friend, I pretend my father is a rich lawyer who works abroad. She invites me to a very glamorous birthday party. I persuade my parents to buy me a new dress.	I go to the friend's massive house. She says we are going to the party in a limo. The limo turns up and my dad is driving. He is a taxi driver and is driving the limo to make extra money so I can go to uni.	I am too embarrassed to tell the truth. I rush into the house and pretend to be sick. Then I go home.

a Can you think of a more satisfying ending? Write (✐) **one or two** sentences explaining your ideas.

....

....

....

....

b How could you describe the friend in a way that will show, not tell, that she is rich? Try writing (✐) **one or two** sentences of description.

....

....

....

....

c Think about which part of the story would make the most engaging opening. Write (✐) the first **one or two** sentences of the story.

....

....

....

....

Your turn!

You are now going to plan your response to this exam-style task.

Exam-style question

Write about a time when you, or someone you know, told a lie.

Your response could be real or imagined.

(40 marks)

1 Use the following questions to come up with ideas. 🖉   For more help with ideas, see Unit 1.

a Who will tell the lie? ....

b Why will they tell a lie? ....

....

c Who are your main characters? ....

d What is your main event? ....

e What type of ending will you have? ....

....

2 Use this three-part structure to plan 🖉 your story.

Beginning	Middle	End

3 Now think about the opening of your story. Will you start with mystery, action or conflict? Explain 🖉 your ideas.

....

....

....

4 Look at the ending of your story. Write 🖉 **one or two** sentences explaining how it will satisfy your readers.

....

....

....

5 Think about your characters. Use the 'show not tell' technique to write 🖉 **two** sentences that will make one of them believable to your readers.

....

....

....

Review your skills

Check up

Review your response to the exam-style question on page 23. Tick ✓ the column to show how well you think you have done each of the following.

	Not quite ✓	Nearly there ✓	Got it! ✓
ended my story effectively	☐	☐	☐
developed interesting characters	☐	☐	☐
thought of a good opening	☐	☐	☐

Look over all of your work in this unit. Note ✎ down **three** ways that you can make your writing more engaging to a reader.

1. ....

2. ....

3. ....

Need more practice?

Plan your response to the exam-style question below.

Exam-style question

Write a story about an occasion when you, or someone you know, found something valuable.

Your response could be real or imagined.

(40 marks)

How confident do you feel about each of these **skills?** Colour ✎ in the bars.

① How do I end my story effectively?

② How do I develop interesting characters?

③ How do I think of a good opening?

④ Structuring your ideas – transactional writing

This unit will help you structure your ideas for a transactional writing task. The skills you will build are to:

- organise your points into a logical order
- plan an effective opening
- plan an effective conclusion.

In the exam, you will be asked to tackle writing tasks such as the one below. This unit will prepare you to write your own response to this question.

Exam-style question

A broadsheet newspaper has published an article titled 'Reality TV: an expensive waste of time'.

You decide to write to the editor giving your views about reality TV.

In your letter, you could discuss:

- the different types of reality TV
- why people watch reality TV
- your views about whether reality TV is a waste of time

as well as any other ideas you might have.

(40 marks)

The three key questions in the **skills boosts** will help you to structure your ideas when writing to present a viewpoint.

① **How do I organise my ideas into a logical order?**

② **How do I write an effective introduction?**

③ **How do I write an effective conclusion?**

Look at one student's plan for a similar task on page 26.

Write a speech to be given at your local school, exploring the value of exams in schools.

Introduction	Exams are not good for everybody.
1	Everybody hates exams at school. Revising means you don't do enough sport and you get unhealthy.
2	Exams cause great stress, many young people get ill, families struggle to cope. Use personal experience about own stress at school.
3	Exams don't teach you important things like how to manage money or get on with people. Use facts about young people having trouble with money.
4	Exams are only good for really clever people. They make more practical students feel a failure. Use examples of friends.
Conclusion	Exams don't benefit all young people.

Look carefully at the plan above. The student has developed the key ideas with interesting details. Now think about the opening, the ending and the order of the points.

1 Which of these statements about the introduction do you most agree with? Tick ✓ your choice.

i. The introduction is interesting and clearly shows the views of the writer. ☐

ii. The introduction is dull and the audience will think the rest of the speech will be boring. ☐

iii. The introduction is effective as it is best to save your good points for the first paragraph. ☐

2 **a** Which of these statements about the conclusion do you most agree with? Tick ✓ your choice.

i. Sum up the writer's feelings and leave a lasting impression. ☐

ii. Just repeat the ideas in the introduction. ☐

b Write 🖉 a better idea for a conclusion.

....

....

3 Is the sequence of ideas logical and would it make the speech interesting? Write 🖉 **two** sentences explaining your thoughts about the sequence.

....

....

....

....

....

1 How do I organise my ideas into a logical order?

To make your transactional writing interesting for a reader, you need to think about where to put your strongest ideas. The sequence of your ideas also needs to be logical.

Look at this exam-style question.

Exam-style question

A broadsheet newspaper has published an article titled 'Reality TV: an expensive waste of time'.

You decide to write to the editor giving your views about reality TV.

Now look at one student's plan for this task. The student has sequenced the plan by adding numbers to each idea.

③ 'Airport' and '24 hours in A&E' are important. Show how places work behind the scenes.
Helps people understand important issues.

① Gives families someting to share. Better than living on smartphones. My family enjoys watching 'Celebrity Lifestyles'.

Reality TV

② Gives chances for ordinary people to be on TV. Many entertainers wouldn't get a chance without shows like 'Britains Got Talent'.

④ Not all about celebrities, some shows are educational, like 'Life on Benefits'. Important to learn about other people's lives.

(1) It is a good idea to start and finish with a strong point.

   a Which **two** are the strongest points in the plan above?

   Renumber them 1 and 4 in the boxes on the plan.

   b Write **one** sentence explaining why the point you have chosen as number 1 is the strongest.

   ....

   ....

   ....

   ....

(2) a Now look at the two remaining points. Decide which should be the second point and which the third by renumbering them on the plan.

   b Write **one** sentence explaining the final order you have used.

   ....

   ....

   ....

   ....

② How do I write an effective introduction?

To engage your reader, you will need to make sure your opening sentence really grabs their attention. To do this, you could use:

- a rhetorical question
- a strong statement that makes your views clear
- a shocking fact or statistic.

The most important thing is to make sure your opening suits your audience, purpose and format.

① Look at these exam-style writing tasks. Think about the audience, purpose and format for each task, then draw a line ✏ linking each one to the most suitable opening.

Write a review of a reality TV show you have seen recently.	Have you ever thought about what it is like to be famous?
A broadsheet newspaper has published an article titled 'Reality TV: an expensive waste of time'. You decide to write to the editor giving your views about reality TV.	75% of reality TV shows are about vain, self-obsessed celebrities.
Write a speech to be given at your school or college encouraging your audience to take part in a reality TV show.	Not all reality TV is about vain, self-obsessed celebrities.

Now look again at this exam-style question you saw earlier in the unit.

Exam-style question

Write a speech to be given at your local school, exploring the value of exams in schools.

② Write ✏ **three** possible openings for your response using **three** different techniques.

Rhetorical question: ....

....

Shocking or interesting fact or statistic: ....

....

Strong statement showing your point of view: ....

....

③ Openings that start, 'I am writing to...' are often boring, but there is one type of exam task that needs this style of opening. Tick ✓ the **one** you think should start this way.

A. | A letter applying for a job | ☐
B. | A report about school catering | ☐
C. | A chapter for a text book | ☐

3 How do I write an effective conclusion?

Your final paragraph should leave your reader with a lasting impression.

Look at these ideas for the conclusion to the exam-style task about reality TV.

End with a warning	Reality TV ruins real life for young people.	☐
End with a question	Do you want to end up as a boring couch potato?	☐
End by asking the audience to take action	Don't just sit there. Turn off the TV and get outside!	☐

1. a Which of these conclusions do you think would be most effective for a speech to young people? Tick ✓ it.

   b Which do you think would be most effective for an article in a broadsheet newspaper? Underline Ⓐ it.

Look again at the following exam-style task.

Exam-style question

Write a speech to be given at your local school, exploring the value of exams in schools.

2. Use each of the techniques above to write 🖉 a conclusion to your response.

   A warning: ....

   ....

   ....

   A question: ....

   ....

   ....

   Asking the audience to take action: ....

   ....

   ....

3. Which of your conclusions do you think would be **most effective**? Write 🖉 **one** sentence explaining your choice.

   ....

   ....

   ....

Sample response

To structure your transactional writing effectively, you should think about:

- the order of your points, particularly your strongest ideas
- using a strong opening that suits your audience, purpose and format
- ending your writing on a strong note that leaves a lasting impression.

Now look at this plan for the writing task about reality TV from the start of the unit.

> *Introduction:* Reality TV is bad
>
> 1.   A lot of the celebrities have no talent. They just do reality TV.
> 2.   Causes a lot of stress. People try to live like the celebrities.
> 3.   Reality TV can be cruel. People are mocked on talent shows.
>
> *Conclusion:*   Warn about dangers to young people.

(1) Rate ✏ the following elements of the student plan out of 5. Explain ✏ your rating in each case.

| The introduction | /5 |

....

....

| The order of the points | /5 |

....

....

| The conclusion | /5 |

....

....

(2) What could this student do to improve the plan? Make ✏ **two** suggestions:

i. ....

....

....

ii. ....

....

....

Your turn!

You are now going to plan your response to this exam-style task.

Exam-style question

A broadsheet newspaper has published an article titled 'Reality TV: an expensive waste of time'.

You decide to write to the editor giving your views about reality TV.

In your letter, you could discuss:

• the different types of reality TV

• why people watch reality TV

• your views about whether reality TV is a waste of time

as well as any other ideas you might have.

(40 marks)

Use the activities below to help you plan your response.

1 **a** Underline Ⓐ key words in the question that show the audience, purpose and format.

b Make notes 🖉 to plan for the audience, purpose and format you have identified.

....

....

....

2 **a** Now use the key words in the question to come up with some ideas 🖉. Use the bullets in the exam-style question to help you.

....

....

....

....

....

....

b Add 🖉 details like facts, statistics or personal experiences to your ideas.

c Draw 🖉 a line through any points that are weak or repetitive.

3 Which of your points is the strongest? Number 🖉 them in order of importance.

4 Write 🖉 an engaging introduction that will grab the attention of your reader.

....

....

....

5 Now plan 🖉 a conclusion that will leave a lasting impression.

....

....

....

Review your skills

Check up

Review your response to the exam-style question on page 31. Tick ✓ the column to show how well you think you have done each of the following.

	Not quite ✓	Nearly there ✓	Got it! ✓
organised my ideas into a logical order	☐	☐	☐
written an effective introduction	☐	☐	☐
written an effective conclusion	☐	☐	☐

Look over all of your work in this unit. Note ✏ down **three** things that you should remember to do when structuring your writing to express a point of view.

1. ....

2. ....

3. ....

Need more practice?

Plan your response to the exam-style question below.

Exam-style question

Write the text for a speech you will give to your peers, encouraging them to take up a healthy lifestyle.

In your speech, you could explain:

• why a healthy lifestyle is important

• why people find a healthy lifestyle difficult

• how to lead a healthy lifestyle

as well as any other ideas you might have.

(40 marks)

How confident do you feel about each of these **skills?** Colour ✏ in the bars.

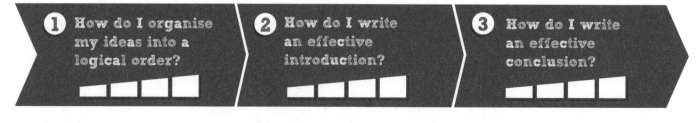

① How do I organise my ideas into a logical order?

② How do I write an effective introduction?

③ How do I write an effective conclusion?

⑤ Making your meaning clear – sentences

This unit will help you to express your ideas clearly. The skills you will build are to:

- start and end your sentences correctly to make your meaning clear
- join your sentences together to develop your ideas
- use punctuation to make your meaning clear.

In the exams, you will be asked to tackle writing tasks like the ones below. This unit will prepare you to write your own response to one of these questions.

Paper 1

Exam-style question

Write about a time when you, or someone you know, made a serious mistake.

Your response could be real or imagined.   (40 marks)

Paper 2

Exam-style question

Write a speech for an audience of young people in which you give your views on the importance of winning.

In your speech, you could consider:

• different types of winning

• the advantages of winning or having winners

• whether winning is always important

as well as any other ideas you might have.   (40 marks)

The three key questions in the **skills boosts** will help you to make your meaning clear.

1 How do I start and end a sentence?

2 How do I join my ideas into longer sentences?

3 How do I use punctuation correctly?

Now read one student's response to the Paper 1 exam-style writing tasks on page 33.

Paper 1

Exam-style question

Write about a time when you, or someone you know, made a serious mistake.

Your response could be real or imagined.

(40 marks)

> My mistake was to move to the city from the country, where I grew up surrounded by the sounds and smells of nature, with lots of friends and family around me. When I left school I moved to the city to a job in a large jewellery shop I thought would be exciting but it was just a confusing deafening place, I had to leave all my friends behind, I was lonely, convinced I would never feel at home.

(1) Read the response carefully and annotate ✐ the sentences. Think about:

a the length of the sentences (Are they too long to make the meaning clear? Look at the sentence beginning 'When I left school...', for example.)

b whether the punctuation helps to make the meaning clear.

Now read another student's response to the Paper 2 exam-style writing task on page 33.

Paper 2

Exam-style question

Write a speech for an audience of young people in which you give your views on the importance of winning.

In your speech, you could consider:

• different types of winning

• the advantages of winning or having winners

• whether winning is always important

as well as any other ideas you might have.

(40 marks)

> Do you think winning is important. I think it is very important! It teaches people valuable skills like resilience and perseverance! My friend Barry works at a Fast Food restaurant. The restaurant has a competition every month to see who sell's the most burger's. Barrys obsessed with winning so he works even harder than usual. Without the competition barry tells me he would find the job dull repetitive and lacking in challenge.

(2) Read the response carefully and annotate ✐ the sentences. Pay attention to:

a the use of capital letters

b the punctuation at the end of sentences

c the use of apostrophes

d whether any sentences could be joined together to make the meaning clearer.

How do I start and end a sentence?

You must start all your sentences with a capital letter and end them with a full stop, an exclamation mark or a question mark. A common error with sentences is using a comma to join two pieces of information instead of a full stop to separate them.

When you want to give the reader two pieces of information, you can do **two** things.

- Separate them with a **full stop**:

My first mistake was to move to the city. It was a deafening, confusing and very unfamiliar place.

- Join them with a **linking word**:

My first mistake was to move to the city __as__ it was a deafening, confusing and very unfamiliar place.

You **cannot** join them with a comma:

~~My first mistake was to move to the city, it was a deafening, confusing and very unfamiliar place.~~

(1) Cross out ✏ the commas in this response and join or separate ✏ the sentences correctly, using a conjunction or a full stop:

I loved my job in the city, I worked in a large fashion store and loved meeting lots of different people. I should never have moved to the country, I had to leave all my friends behind. The countryside was very green and peaceful, it was sometimes too quiet.

Exclamation marks can be used to end a sentence if you want to show excitement or danger.

Be careful: too many exclamation marks can mean they lose their impact.

(2) Add ✏ an exclamation mark to **one** of these sentences to add a sense of excitement.

One of my biggest mistakes in the country was not to listen to warnings about animals. I wanted to make the most of nature so I explored for hours every day. Many of the fields were full of what I thought were cows. I only found out they were bulls when one charged at me. They had all looked friendly from a distance.

(3) The student who wrote the following response has used too many exclamation marks and has also forgotten a question mark and a capital letter. Correct ✏ the mistakes and leave ✏ just **one** exclamation mark.

I always want to win even if I am just playing Monopoly with my mates! who doesn't want to win. Those who say winning doesn't matter are just losers! They probably just don't want to try hard at anything! Competition is good for you as you learn something even if you don't come first.

How do I join my ideas into longer sentences?

To make your writing more interesting and develop your meaning, you can join simple sentences together to make longer ones. You can do this by using linking words such as 'and', 'or', 'but', 'because', 'although', 'unless', 'if', etc. These each have different effects and help to serve your intention.

You can join simple sentences together to make your meaning clear.

- Use 'but' or 'although' to show that there are two different points of view:

> *Winning is very important to most people __although__ there are some who think taking part is more important...*

- Use 'and' to join two points, or to add a point:

> *...__and__ I agree with them...*

- Use 'because' or 'as' to explain your point:

> *...__because__ it teaches valuable lessons.*

- Use 'or' to show alternative ideas:

> *Sport can be played to win __or__ it can simply be played for fun...*

- Use 'so' to show the consequence of your point:

> *...__so__ it's quite easy to take some exercise...*

- Use 'if' or 'unless' to add a condition to your point:

> *...__unless__ you want to end up as a couch potato!*

(1) **a** Look at these simple sentences from one student's response about winning. Join ✏ the first sentence to each of the others by choosing one of the linking words to make your meaning clear.

and	or	as	although	but

Taking part in competitions is good for you.		Competing can teach you valuable skills like perseverance and resilience.
		Not everybody thinks winning is important.
		You can just play sport for enjoyment.

b Now look at these simple sentences from another student's response about losing. Think about the meaning you want to convey. Join ✏ the first sentence to each of the others by using one of the linking words.

if	or	so	and	because

We all need to learn what it is like to lose.		Competitive sport is very important.
		We want to appreciate the joy of winning.
		I personally have never won a single race.

3 How do I use punctuation correctly?

You should use punctuation correctly to make your meaning clear or help develop your meaning. Commas can be used to separate information within a sentence.

You can use commas to add extra information in the form of a list.

For example you can add a list of:

adjectives	noun phrases
He was tall, smartly dressed and very good-looking.	My friend won the essay competition at school, the player of the year title at football and the best dressed award at the Summer Prom.

(1) Complete ✐ these sentences by listing information using **commas**.

    a   Add **adjectives**: The weather was ....

          ....

    b   Add **noun phrases**: We all need to learn ....

          ....

You can also add extra information to a sentence by using one of these **pronouns**.

that	who	which
whose	where	when

For example:

The house always looked dark and frightening.	The house, <u>which</u> stood on the top of a steep hill, always looked dark and frightening.	Notice how the additional information appears between **commas**.
My brother thinks that winning is the most important thing in the world.	My brother, <u>who</u> plays professional football, thinks that winning is the most important thing in the world.	

(2) Practise adding ✐ information to these sentences using **pronouns** from the table above.

Remember to place the new information between **commas**.

    a   My friend told me I was making a big mistake.
        My friend, ...

        ...., told me I was making a big mistake.

    b   It was at the park that I made my first mistake.
        It was at the park, ...

        ...., that I made my first mistake.

    c   My first football trophy stands on the mantelpiece.
        My first football trophy, ...

        ...., stands on the mantelpiece.

Sample response

To make the meaning of your sentences clear, you need to think about:

- the way you start and end sentences
- joining simple sentences together to make your writing more interesting
- using commas to add extra detail to your sentences.

Look at the paragraph below from one student's response to this exam-style writing task from page 33.

Exam-style question

Write about a time when you, or someone you know, made a serious mistake.

Your response could be real or imagined.

(40 marks)

> My big mistake was telling everything to my friend Alice! Alice was the perfect friend. We did everything together. I thought she was the kindest funniest person I had ever met. As we grew up we shared clothes make-up and even our deepest secrets about everything. When I met John at tennis lessons I told Alice how much I liked him. I knew she would want to meet him. I didn't think she would want him for herself!

(1) How could the sentences be improved to develop the writer's meaning? Redraft 🖉 the paragraph in the space below, thinking carefully about these ideas.

- Can extra detail be added to any sentence? (Perhaps something about Alice or John?)
- Are both exclamation marks adding meaning?
- Are any commas missing?
- Can any sentences be joined together to form longer sentences that develop the writer's meaning?

....

....

....

....

....

....

....

....

....

....

....

....

Your turn!

Choose one of the two exam-style tasks you saw at the beginning of this unit.

> **Exam-style question**
>
> Write about a time when you, or someone you know, made a serious mistake.
>
> Your response could be real or imagined. **(40 marks)**

> **Exam-style question**
>
> Write a speech for an audience of young people in which you give your views on the importance of winning.
>
> In your speech, you could consider:
> - different types of winning
> - the advantages of winning or having winners
> - whether winning is always important
>
> as well as any other ideas you might have. **(40 marks)**

You are going to **plan** and **write** the first two paragraphs of your response, focusing on sentence structure and punctuation.

(**1**) Use this space to note down ✐ all the different ideas for your response.

(**2**) (**a**) Choose the ideas that you will focus on in your opening two paragraphs. Tick ✓ them.

(**b**) Think about any extra details you could add to the ideas for these two paragraphs. Make a note ✐ of them below.

(**3**) Now write ✐ the first two paragraphs of your response on paper, thinking carefully about:
- the way you start and end sentences
- joining simple sentences together to make your writing more interesting
- using commas to add detail to your sentences.

Review your skills

Check up

Review your response to the exam-style question on page 39. Tick ✓ the column to show how well you think you have done each of the following.

	Not quite ✓	Nearly there ✓	Got it! ✓
started and ended a sentence	☐	☐	☐
joined my ideas into longer sentences	☐	☐	☐
used punctuation correctly	☐	☐	☐

Look over all of your work in this unit. Note down 🖉 **three** things you can do to improve your sentences.

1. ....

2. ....

3. ....

Need more practice?

You could either:

• add a paragraph to your response to the task you chose on page 39

or:

• tackle the other writing task on page 39.

How confident do you feel about each of these **skills?** Colour 🖉 in the bars.

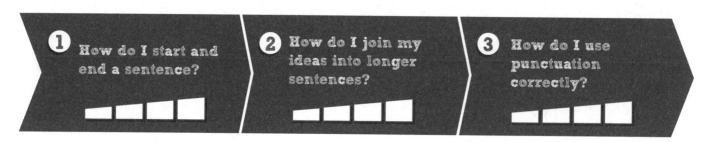

❶ How do I start and end a sentence?

❷ How do I join my ideas into longer sentences?

❸ How do I use punctuation correctly?

⑥ Writing sentences to create impact

This unit will help you write sentences that create impact. The skills you will build are to:

- open your sentences in a variety of interesting ways
- structure your sentences in a variety of interesting ways
- use short minor sentences to create impact.

In the exam, you will be asked to tackle writing tasks like the ones below. This unit will prepare you to write your own response to one of these questions.

Paper 1

Exam-style question

Write about a time when you, or someone you know, received bad news.

Your response could be real or imagined.

(40 marks)

Paper 2

Exam-style question

A newspaper has published an article with the title 'Donating to charity is a waste of time'.
You decide to write to the editor, giving your views about donating money to charity.

In your letter you could include:

- what types of charity exist and why they need money
- your views about why people donate to charity
- things that people could do to help charities rather than giving money

as well as any other ideas you might have.

(40 marks)

The three key questions in the **skills boosts** will help you to write sentences to create impact.

 1 How do I open my sentences to create impact?

 2 How do I structure my sentences to create impact?

 3 How do I use short sentences to create impact?

Look at extracts from one student's answers to the exam-style tasks above on page 42.

Paper 1

Exam-style question

Write about a time when you, or someone you know, received bad news.

> I was driving us home from the party when she told me the bad news. The radio was very loud and Sarah was humming along to a tune she likes. She stopped humming and mumbled something quietly. I didn't hear her at first so she said it again loudly. I turned to stare at her when I finally realised what she was telling me. I took my eyes off the road for too long and crashed the car into a tree.

(1) Which of the following would give this paragraph more impact? Tick ✓ **two.**

A.	Using a variety of different words to open each sentence.
B.	Using a short sentence to create tension about the car crashing.
C.	Starting each sentence with the pronoun 'I'.
D.	Using very long sentences to add lots of detail.

Paper 2

Exam-style question

A newspaper has published an article with the title 'Donating to charity is a waste of time'. You decide to write to the editor, giving your views about donating money to charity.

> Some people give money to charity because they feel guilty for having a nice life. Other people give to charity because they have somebody in their family who is ill or needs help. Some people give to many charities because they are lucky enough to have too much money to spend on themselves.

(2) Which statement best describes the sentences in this paragraph? Tick ✓ **one.**

A.	The sentences use a variety of structures to create impact.
B.	The sentences use a variety of openings to create impact.
C.	The paragraph lacks impact as the sentences are all similar in structure.
D.	The sentences are all too short to create impact.

1 How do I open my sentences to create impact?

Thinking about the first word of a sentence can create impact and make your writing more interesting to read. You can start a sentence with any of these.

Type of word	Examples
A pronoun (a word which stands in the place of a noun) I, you, he, she, it, we, they, my, your, his, her, our, their	**I** crashed the car when I heard...
A preposition (a word which tells you the position of something or someone) above, behind, between, near, with, on, under	**Between us** blared the radio, which drowned out Sarah's words...
An 'ing' verb (an action word) running, hurrying, waiting, holding	**Raising** money for charity can make people feel...
An adjective (a describing word) slow, quiet, large, huge	**Huge** amounts of money are raised each year...
An adverb (a word that describes a verb) alarmingly, painfully, happily, quickly	**Surprisingly,** over 50% of people never give any money to charity... If you use an adverb at the start of a sentence, remember to put a comma after it.

(1) Write **five** sentences about giving money to charity. For each one, use a different opening from the table above.

i. ....

....

ii. ....

....

iii. ....

....

iv. ....

....

v. ....

....

How do I structure my sentences to create impact?

Structuring your sentences in different ways can change the impact of your ideas.

Read the sentences below in which a student writes about people who donate to charity.

This sentence makes people's **laziness** the most important idea as it is positioned towards the end of the sentence:

> People donate to charity out of guilt because they are too lazy to do anything practical to help others.

This sentence emphasises people's **guilt** as this information comes at the end of the sentence:

> People are too lazy to do anything practical to help others so they donate to charity out of guilt.

(1) Change the structure of this sentence to make **poverty** the most important point. Write 🖉 your new version here.

> The government would have to do more about poverty if we all stopped donating to charity.

....

....

(2) The impact of a sentence can be changed by varying the position of the information within it. Look at these two versions of a sentence in which a student writes about receiving bad news.

Version 1

> [1] I turned to stare at her [2] when I finally realised what she was telling me [3] and took my eyes off the road for too long.

Version 2

> [2] When I finally realised what she was telling me [1] I turned to stare at her [3] and took my eyes off the road for too long.

a Practise 🖉 restructuring the sentence in **two** more ways.

Version 3 ....

....

....

Version 4 ....

....

....

b Which version (including your own) creates the most impact? Circle (A) it. Write 🖉 **one** sentence explaining your choice.

....

....

③ How do I use short sentences to create impact?

Short sentences can be particularly effective when you want to add impact to an argument or tension to a story.

Look at this student's paragraph in response to the Paper 2-style question on page 41 about donating to charity.

> Many charities rely on donations to provide help to those most in need. It is often only because of charity organisations that children in poorer countries have access to clean water, healthy food and vaccinations. Without these charities, many thousands of children would die each day. Our donations keep them alive.

Here the final short sentence adds **impact** as it follows several longer sentences.

① Practise using short sentences by adding ✐ **two** sentences to the following paragraph. Make **one** of your sentences short, to add impact.

> It is often only because of charity donations that children in poorer countries have access to clean water, healthy food and vaccinations. Many people feel helping those abroad is wrong as we have children in this country who need help.

....

....

....

....

....

Now look at how a short sentence can be used to add **tension** to a story.

> My heart began to race, blood rushed into my ears and my vision went blurry. My stomach was churning and I could feel my legs shaking. As I stared into the gloom I could just see the door beginning to open in the distance. I froze.

② Practise using short sentences to add tension by replacing ✐ the last two sentences above with **two** of your own.

> My heart began to race, blood rushed into my ears and my vision went blurry. My stomach was churning and I could feel my legs shaking.

....

....

....

....

....

....

Sample response

To write sentences that create impact and are interesting to read you need to think about:

- using a variety of words at the start of your sentences
- how you structure your sentences
- using short sentences to create impact or tension.

Now look at this exam-style task which you saw at the beginning of the unit.

Exam-style question

Write about a time when you, or someone you know, received bad news.

Your response could be real or imagined.

(40 marks)

> It had started as just an ordinary day for me. When the bombshell was dropped I was just drumming my fingers on the steering wheel, concentrating on the heavy traffic ahead and thinking about what to have for dinner. Mumbling quietly under her breath, Sarah gave me the bad news. I turned to stare at her when I finally realised what she was telling me. The steering wheel slipped from my grasp as dancing stars appeared in front of my eyes and blood rushed into my ears. I crashed the car.

① Read the extract from one student's response above. Try reading it aloud so that you can hear the impact of the sentences. Then annotate 🖉 the paragraph, making notes about the effectiveness of:

   ⓐ **the sentence openings**: are they varied and do they create impact?

   ⓑ **the sentence structures**: could any sentences be restructured to create more impact?

   ⓒ **the final short sentence**: how does it create impact?

② Can you think of an alternative final sentence? Write 🖉 it below.

....

....

....

....

Your turn!

Choose **one** of the two exam-style tasks you saw at the beginning of this unit.

Paper 1

Exam-style question

Write about a time when you, or someone you know, received bad news.

Your response could be real or imagined. (40 marks)

Paper 2

Exam-style question

A newspaper has published an article with the title 'Donating to charity is a waste of time'.
You decide to write to the editor, giving your views about donating money to charity.

In your letter you could include:

• what types of charity exist and why they need money

• your views about why people donate to charity

• things that people could do to help charities rather than giving money

as well as any other ideas you might have. (40 marks)

You are going to plan and write the first **two** paragraphs of your response. You should focus on writing sentences that create impact.

(1) Use the box below to note down 🖉 some ideas. (Space your notes out so you can add more detail later.)

(2) Tick ✓ the ideas that you will focus on in your two paragraphs. Make sure you have added enough detail to the ideas you have chosen. Add 🖉 more if necessary.

(3) Now write 🖉 your **two** paragraphs on paper, thinking carefully about:

• the words you use at the start of your sentences

• the way you structure your sentences

• using short sentences to create impact.

Review your skills

Check up

Review your response to the exam-style question you chose on page 47. Tick ✓ the column to show how well you think you have done each of the following.

	Not quite ✓	Nearly there ✓	Got it! ✓
opened my sentences to create impact	☐	☐	☐
structured my sentences to create impact	☐	☐	☐
used short sentences to create impact	☐	☐	☐

Look over all of your work in this unit. Note down ✏ **three** ways you can add impact to your sentences.

1. ....

2. ....

3. ....

Need more practice?

You could either:

• add a paragraph to the task you chose on page 47

or:

• tackle the other writing task on page 47.

Remember to focus on creating impact through your choice of sentence structure.

How confident do you feel about each of these **skills?** Colour ✏ in the bars.

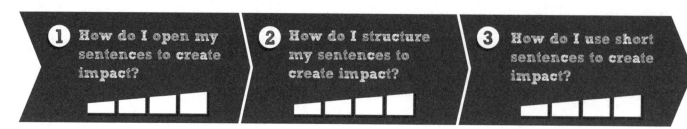

1 How do I open my sentences to create impact?

2 How do I structure my sentences to create impact?

3 How do I use short sentences to create impact?

(7) Writing paragraphs to create impact

This unit will help you write paragraphs that will create impact and make your meaning clear. The skills you will build are to:

- use clear paragraphs to separate your ideas
- structure and develop your paragraphs to make your meaning clear
- structure your paragraphs to create impact.

In the exam, you will be asked to tackle writing tasks like the ones below. This unit will prepare you to write your own response to one of these questions.

Paper 1

Exam-style question

Write about a time when you, or someone you know, had an unexpected visitor.

Your response could be real or imagined. (40 marks)

Paper 2

Exam-style question

Write an article for a community newspaper, exploring the idea that all schools should include one hour of physical education every day.

In your article, you could write about:

- the benefits of taking regular exercise
- the alternatives to exercising at school
- the advantages/disadvantages of making all students exercise at school

as well as any other ideas you might have. (40 marks)

The three key questions in the **skills boosts** will help you to write paragraphs to create impact and make your meaning clear.

1 How do I start paragraphs?

2 How do I structure my paragraphs to make my meaning clear?

3 How do I structure my paragraphs to create impact?

Look at the extracts on page 50 from two students' answers to the exam-style tasks above.

Paper 1

Exam-style question

Write about a time when you, or someone you know, had an unexpected visitor.
Your response could be real or imagined.

(40 marks)

> Ben jumped up in shock because a loud knock at the door woke him. He crept slowly into the hall and reached for his doorkeys. He wondered who was calling so late on a weeknight.

① Is this paragraph structured so that it creates impact? Write ✏ a sentence explaining your answer.

....

....

....

Paper 2

Exam-style question

Write an article for a community newspaper, exploring the idea that all schools should include one hour of physical education every day.

> Teenagers spend most of their lives in front of a computer screen. Many teenagers, particularly boys, spend hours playing computer games. Girls spend hours on the internet. This can lead to depression and isolation. Most teenagers do not take the recommended amount of exercise each day. I see young people catch the bus to school even if they live close enough to walk. Most children do not take part in any organised sports. This is increasing teenage obesity.

② This student has two different ideas but they have all been put into one long paragraph. Each new idea or point should have a new paragraph. Mark ✏ where a new idea has been introduced.

③ What is the topic of each paragraph in the student's response? Complete ✏ the sentences.

   ⓐ Paragraph 1 is about ....

....

....

....

   ⓑ Paragraph 2 is about ....

....

....

....

④ Each paragraph should be developed with evidence. In the student answer above, underline Ⓐ the sentences that contain evidence.

How do I start paragraphs?

You need to use paragraphs to organise your points and make it easier for your readers to follow your ideas.

For transactional writing, you should start a new paragraph each time you start a new point. Each paragraph should start with a sentence that clearly introduces the content of the paragraph. This is called a topic sentence. For example:

> <u>Our school makes a big effort to encourage teenagers to take exercise</u>. All students are given time after lunch to take part in organised activities such as football, basketball and gymnastics. The school also has many sports teams that train after school. Even the staff play 5-a-side football, although they are usually beaten!

(1) Add ✎ a topic sentence to this paragraph from a student's response to the exam-style question on page 50.

....

....

> Most teenagers catch the bus to school, use escalators instead of stairs and rely on their parents for lifts rather than walking anywhere. Behind my house is a school and the road is blocked every day with parents dropping off or collecting children who live less than a mile away. This is increasing teenage obesity.

For imaginative writing, it is a good idea to start a new paragraph:

• when you move forwards or backwards in time
• when you move to a new setting
• when you introduce a new character, or change to another point of view.

For example:

> Ben settled back in his chair in front of the fire. It had been a long day and all Ben could think about was his aching back, his sore feet and his frozen hands. Finally, he was able to sit down and relax. Sighing happily, Ben closed his eyes for a sleep.
>
> Outside, heavy rain was battering against the windows and wind was howling through the trees. Leaves blew around the garden. The surface of the pond was beginning to freeze over and icicles were starting to form on the roof.

(2) Practise writing ✎ **two** different opening sentences to the next paragraph of this story by moving forwards or backwards in time, or by introducing a new character.

i. ....

....

....

ii. ....

....

....

Unit 7 Writing paragraphs to create impact   51

② How do I structure my paragraphs to make my meaning clear?

For transactional writing, it is important to structure your writing clearly to make your meaning clear. One way to do this is to use a Point–Evidence–Explain (P.E.E.) structure:

- A clear **point** should be made in the topic sentence.
- **Evidence** should then be used to prove the point. Evidence can be facts, statistics or examples.
- An **explanation** should then be given to link the evidence to the point.

① Look at this student's paragraph in response to the exam-style question on page 49.

> Teenage obesity is a big problem in the UK. A recent survey showed that eighty-five percent of teenagers do not take the recommended daily amount of exercise. Instead of playing sports outside, they are spending all their time in front of a computer screen. This inactivity will make the obesity situation a lot worse if we do nothing.

Underline Ⓐ the **point**, the **evidence** and the **explanation** in the above paragraph.

② ⓐ Complete ✎ these P.E.E. paragraphs by adding evidence and an explanation that links your evidence to the point. Try to add interest by including **more than one** piece of evidence.

Exercise at school does not have to be boring.

Daily exercise has many benefits.

ⓑ Now underline Ⓐ the **point**, the **evidence** and the **explanation** in your paragraphs.

③ Look at your evidence. Have you stuck to facts and statistics? Using a personal experience can add interest. Rewrite ✎ **one** of your paragraphs, using a personal experience instead of facts.

3 How do I structure my paragraphs to create impact?

For imaginative writing, you should structure your paragraphs to create impact. You can do this by:
- building up to a moment of tension, action or drama
- using a one sentence paragraph to create suspense.

① In an imaginative text, you can structure a paragraph to build up to a moment of tension or drama. Number ✐ these sentences in order to create a structure that would produce tension.

	He froze.
	Ben's heart banged in his chest as he heard a sudden knocking at the door.
	Standing in front of him was a man who was supposed to be dead.
	His palms were sweaty and his breathing came in gasps.
	Slowly he opened the door and peered out.

② A paragraph can consist of just one sentence. Very short paragraphs can create impact by emphasising a point or creating suspense. Look again at the sentences above. Which sentence could be separated from the rest to create a short paragraph for extra impact? Write ✐ **one** sentence explaining your choice.

....

....

③ Now look at this variation on the paragraph you read on page 51.

It had been a long and tiring day. All Ben could think about was his aching back, his sore feet and his frozen hands. The doorbell rang just as Ben sat down. Slowly getting to his feet, Ben shuffled towards the door. He opened it wide and looked out into the dark night. On the doorstep was a large black box.

ⓐ Restructure ✐ the paragraph above to create more impact.

....

....

....

....

....

....

....

ⓑ Can you add still more impact by adding ✐ a one-sentence paragraph?

....

....

....

Sample response

To write paragraphs that create impact you need to think about:

- using a new paragraph for each new idea
- using topic sentences and a P.E.E. structure to make the meaning of your paragraphs clear in your transactional writing
- structuring your imaginative paragraphs to increase drama or create tension
- using one-sentence paragraphs to emphasise points or create suspense.

Now look at this exam-style writing task, which you saw at the beginning of the unit.

Exam-style question

Write about a time when you, or someone you know, had an unexpected visitor.

Your response could be real or imagined.

(40 marks)

> I was tucked up in bed when the doorbell rang. It was late and we were not expecting any visitors. Doors banged, keys rattled and footsteps sounded as my dad let the visitor in. Listening carefully, I could hear muffled voices coming from the hall.
>
> Getting out of bed, I crept to the top of the stairs. I still couldn't make out exactly what was being said but it sounded bad. Rusty, our German Shepherd, started barking and scratching at the kitchen door. Suddenly, I heard a crash and a cry.
>
> I didn't see my dad again for another five days.

(1) Read the sample answer carefully. Try reading it aloud so that you can hear the impact of the sentences and paragraphs. Then annotate 🖉 the answer, commenting on its effectiveness.

    a Comment on the use of three paragraphs. Why start a new paragraph when the narrator gets out of bed?

    b Comment on the order of the sentences within the paragraphs. How is tension built up?

    c Comment on the use of the single-sentence paragraph at the end. How does this create suspense?

Your turn!

Choose **one** of the two exam-style tasks you saw at the beginning of this unit.

Paper 1

Exam-style question

Write about a time when you, or someone you know, had an unexpected visitor.

Your response could be real or imagined. (40 marks)

Paper 2

Exam-style question

Write an article for a community newspaper, exploring the idea that all schools should include one hour of physical education every day.

In your article, you could write about:

• the benefits of taking regular exercise

• the alternatives to exercising at school

• the advantages/disadvantages of making all students exercise at school

as well as any other ideas you might have. (40 marks)

You are going to plan and write the first three paragraphs of your response.
You should focus on writing paragraphs that create impact.

(1) Use this space to note down ✐ some ideas.

(2) Choose ✓ the ideas that you will focus on in your three paragraphs.
Make sure you have added ✐ detail to your ideas.

(3) Now use paper to write ✐ **three** paragraphs, thinking carefully about:

• when to start a new paragraph

• how you open your paragraphs

• how you structure your paragraphs

• using a one-sentence paragraph to create impact.

Review your skills

Check up

Review your response to the exam-style question on page 55. Tick ⊘ the column to show how well you think you have done each of the following.

	Not quite ⊘	Nearly there ⊘	Got it! ⊘
started paragraphs	☐	☐	☐
structured my sentences to make my meaning clear	☐	☐	☐
structured my paragraphs to create impact	☐	☐	☐

Look over all of your work in this unit. Note down 🖉 **three** things you can do to improve the impact of your paragraphs.

1. ....

2. ....

3. ....

Need more practice?

You could either:

• add a paragraph to your response to the task you chose on page 55

or:

• tackle the other writing task on page 55.

How confident do you feel about each of these **skills?** Colour 🖉 in the bars.

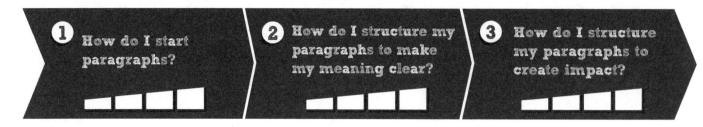

① How do I start paragraphs?

② How do I structure my paragraphs to make my meaning clear?

③ How do I structure my paragraphs to create impact?

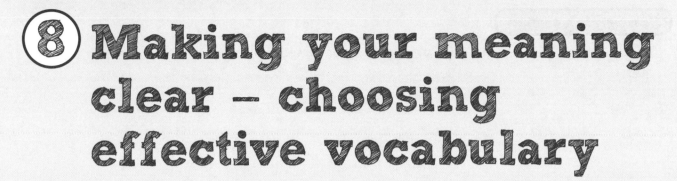

8 Making your meaning clear – choosing effective vocabulary

This unit will help you to select vocabulary that adds impact to your transactional writing. The skills you will build are to:

- select the most effective words to avoid repetition and create impact
- use linking words and phrases to guide readers through your ideas
- use techniques that add impact to your writing.

In the exam, you will be asked to tackle writing tasks such as the one below. This unit will prepare you to write your own response to this question.

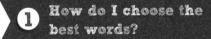

Exam-style question

Write an article for a national newspaper giving your views about experiments on animals.

In your article, you could consider:

- the ways animals are used in experiments
- the benefits of experimenting on animals: for example, finding cures for cancer
- the disadvantages of experimenting on animals

as well as any other ideas you might have.

(40 marks)

The three key questions in the **skills boosts** will help you to create impact by selecting the most effective vocabulary.

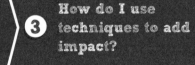

1 How do I choose the best words?

2 How do I link my ideas?

3 How do I use techniques to add impact?

Look at the extract on page 58 from one student's answer to the task above.

Write an article for a national newspaper giving your views about experiments on animals.

A lot of small <u>animals</u> like mice, rats and rabbits are being kept in bad conditions in small cages. The <u>animals</u> just sit in there, waiting for the next experiment to start. The small cages give the <u>animals</u> no room to move around. This causes stress that causes the <u>animals</u> to behave strangely and pull out their hair or bite their nails. When someone walks past the <u>animals'</u> small cages the <u>animals</u> jump because they have learned to be frightened of humans. Do you want to be one of the humans that does this?

1. The word <u>animal</u> has been used too often. Which of the following could have been used in some of the sentences? Tick ✓ them.

	them		us		there
	their		they		it

2. The student has used the phrase small cages three times. This lacks impact. Can you think of alternatives to the word 'small' that would increase the impact? Note down ✎ your ideas.

   ....

3. The student has not clearly signposted the ideas in the paragraph. Annotate ✎ the paragraph to show where you think the linking phrases below could be used to make the paragraph more powerful.

   | In particular | | Consequently | | Furthermore |

4. The paragraph ends with a rhetorical question. How does this add impact? Explain ✎ your thoughts.

   ....

   ....

   ....

   ....

① How do I choose the best words?

Synonyms are words with similar meanings. You can use them in your writing to avoid repetition and to add impact.

① Look at these two versions of a paragraph about experimenting on animals.

> Animals are often used to test cosmetics. For this, animals have chemicals injected into their bodies and mascara put into their eyes. We should stop animals being treated in this way by testing cosmetics on humans instead of on animals.

> Animals are often used to test cosmetics. For this, they have chemicals injected into their bodies and mascara put into their eyes. We should stop them being treated in this way by testing cosmetics on humans instead.

a Underline (A) the changes between the two versions.

b Which version is the most effective? Write (✏) **one** sentence explaining your choice.

....

....

② Synonyms can also be used to add impact to your writing.

☐	Animal testing is bad.
☐	Animal testing is brutal.
☐	Animal testing is horrific.
☐	Animal testing is barbaric.
☐	Animal testing is cruel.

a Which of these sentences would have the most impact on a reader? Number (✏) the above sentences 1–5, with 5 being the greatest impact.

b Now come up with (✏) some synonyms for the highlighted words in this sentence.

> Helpless animals are kept in small cages.

helpless ....

animals ....

kept ....

cages ....

② How do I link my ideas?

To guide your reader through your ideas you should use a range of linking words and phrases. These are called **adverbials**.

① Copy ✎ the adverbials below into the correct box in the table, according to their purpose.

in addition	for instance	in contrast	additionally	in particular
as a result	furthermore	significantly	in conclusion	because
likewise	therefore	secondly	especially	
however	on the other hand	next	firstly	

Adding an idea:	Explaining an idea:	Introducing an example:
Comparing or contrasting ideas:	**Emphasising important ideas:**	**Ordering ideas:**

② Look at these paragraphs of a student's response to the exam-style question about experiments on animals.

...., some people say that an animal's life is not as important as that of a human. ...., it is often said that they only exist so that humans can use them for food. ...., I believe that we should learn to love and look after all small creatures. ...., even rats make excellent pets as they are loyal and loving towards their owners.

...., the animals used for testing are kept in appalling conditions. ...., they are kept alone in tiny cages for most of the day with no light. They are taken out only when they are needed for experiments, all of which are very cruel. ...., they are even kept short of water and fed only enough to keep them alive. ...., many start to pull out their own feathers or fur.

Fill in ✎ the gaps by using appropriate adverbial words or phrases from the boxes above.

3 How do I use techniques to add impact?

Language techniques can be used to add power and impact to your writing.

(1) Look at the examples of students' writing on the left. Draw lines (✐) to match them to the correct techniques on the right.

A. Why should innocent creatures be tortured?

B. All kinds of animals are used including dogs, rabbits, guinea pigs and hamsters.

C. The animals that are used are just like your beloved cat or dog.

D. Keeping small animals alone in cages is cruel. Keeping them without food and water is cruel. Pouring chemicals into their eyes is cruel.

list

rhetorical question

repetition

direct address

(2) Now use each of the techniques above to write (✐) your own sentences in response to the task on page 57 about experiments on animals.

list ....

....

....

rhetorical question ....

....

....

repetition ....

....

....

direct address ....

....

....

Sample response

As you select vocabulary to create impact in your transactional writing, you need to think about:

- using synonyms to avoid repetition
- using adverbials to guide readers through your ideas
- using language techniques that add power to your writing.

Now look at this exam-style question again.

Exam-style question

Write an article for a national newspaper giving your views about experiments on animals.

In your article, you could consider:

- the ways animals are used in experiments
- the benefits of experimenting on animals: for example, finding cures for cancer
- the disadvantages of experimenting on animals

as well as any other ideas you might have.

(40 marks)

Now look at this extract from one student's response to the task.

> Additionally, many of the animals that are killed by experiments are creatures that many people keep as pets. For example, dogs, cats, rabbits and guinea pigs are all hurt so that we can have medicines. In particular, experiments are done on puppies almost as soon as they are born. These puppies are kept in tiny cages. These puppies are kept without food and water for days. These puppies are then cut open before having chemicals put onto them. How would you feel if this were your animal?

(1) Read the student's paragraph aloud. How effective are the vocabulary choices this student has made?

   a Underline (A) any adverbials used to signpost you through the writing. Select **one** adverbial and explain how it helps to add impact to the writing.

     ....

     ....

   b Replace (✎) the highlighted words with words or phrases that have more impact.

   c Explain (✎) how the following add impact to the writing:

     i. A list of small animal types ....

     ....

     ii. Repetition of the word 'puppy' ....

     ....

     iii. Ending with a rhetorical question ....

     ....

Your turn!

You are now going to write three paragraphs of a response to this exam-style task.

Exam-style question

Write an article for a national newspaper giving your views about experiments on animals.

In your article, you could consider:

• the ways animals are used in experiments

• the benefits of experimenting on animals: for example, finding cures for cancer

• the disadvantages of experimenting on animals

as well as any other ideas you might have.

(40 marks)

1 Think about all the different ideas you could include in your response.
   Use the space to note down ✏ some ideas.

2 Choose ✓ the ideas that you will focus on in your three paragraphs.
   Make sure you have added ✏ detail to your ideas.

3 Now write ✏ your response on paper. Remember to focus on:

   • using synonyms to avoid repetition and add impact

   • using adverbials to guide the reader through your ideas

   • using language techniques to add impact.

Review your skills

Check up

Review your response to the exam-style question on page 63. Tick ✓ the column to show how well you think you have done each of the following.

	Not quite ✓	Nearly there ✓	Got it! ✓
chosen the best words	☐	☐	☐
linked my ideas	☐	☐	☐
used techniques to add impact	☐	☐	☐

Look over all of your work in this unit. Note down ✏ **three** ways you can add impact through your vocabulary choices:

1. ....

2. ....

3. ....

Need more practice?

Try tackling the Paper 2 question below.

Exam-style question

Write an article for a magazine exploring the idea that every teenager should have a part-time job.

In your article, you could discuss:

• what types of part-time job teenagers could do

• the advantages/disadvantages of teenagers working part-time

• your views on whether teenagers should have to work part-time

as well as any other ideas you might have.

(40 marks)

How confident do you feel about each of these **skills?** Colour ✏ in the bars.

❶ How do I choose the best words?	❷ How do I link my ideas?	❸ How do I use techniques to add impact?
☐☐☐☐	☐☐☐☐	☐☐☐☐

⑨ Creating impact with vocabulary – imaginative writing

This unit will help you select vocabulary that adds impact to your imaginative writing. The skills you will build are to:

- select words for effect
- use language techniques to create images in your readers' minds
- use the senses to develop your descriptions.

In the exam, you will be asked to tackle writing tasks such as the ones below. This unit will prepare you to write your own response to this question.

Exam-style question

Look at the images provided.

Write about a time when you, or someone you know, went on a day trip.

Your response can be real or imagined.

You may wish to base your response on one of the images. **(40 marks)**

Exam-style question

Write about a time when you, or someone you know, found something hidden.

Your response could be real or imagined. **(40 marks)**

The three key tasks in the **skills boosts** will help you to select vocabulary for impact and effect in your narrative and descriptive writing.

 1 How do I choose words for effect?

2 How do I use language techniques to create images?

 3 How do I review and improve my vocabulary choices?

Look at the extracts from two students' responses on page 66 to the first exam-style task above.

Exam-style question

Write about a time when you, or someone you know, went on a day trip.

Student A

> The sea glistened like a beautiful jewel. Waves lapped gently onto the rocks. Looking up, I was blinded by the sun as it rose like a giant yellow balloon. Scratchy clumps of seaweed stuck to my feet as I strolled down to the emerald green water. I sank slowly onto the soft yellow sand. The beach was a fabulous place to have a day out.

/5

Student B

> The sea looked nice and cool. I could see waves coming in to the beach. The sun was very hot. Seaweed was sticking to my feet as I walked along. I sat down on the sand. I decided that this day out was going to be good fun.

/5

1 Look closely at both extracts. Which do you think has the most effective vocabulary choices? Give 🖉 each one a mark out of 5, using the scale below.

1	Vocabulary choices have no impact.
2	Vocabulary choices have some impact.
3	Vocabulary choices create a picture.
4	Vocabulary choices create a clear picture of the beach.
5	Vocabulary choices create a brilliant picture of the beach.

2 Which of the two student extracts is the most effective? Write 🖉 **one** sentence explaining your choice.

....

....

....

3 Now look again at your choice of extract in question **2**. Underline Ⓐ any vocabulary that you feel is effective. Select **one** example that you have underlined and write 🖉 **one** sentence explaining its effect.

....

....

....

How do I choose words for effect?

You can add impact to your writing by choosing emotive language. Emotive language is vocabulary that creates images in the minds of your readers. To do this, you can:

- use exciting synonyms for verbs
- use adjectives in your descriptions
- use adverbs to add impact to your verbs.

1 Look at the sentence below from one student's description of a beach.

> I saw seagulls flying down on to the sand as I walked along the beach.

Now look at some more exciting synonyms for the verbs in the sentence.

glimpsed	swooping	strolled
watched	soaring	ambled
spied	gliding	strode

....

....

a Add 🖉 one or two more synonyms to each of the columns.

b Practise using alternative verbs in place of those highlighted to add impact to the sentence. Write 🖉 out your sentences.

i. ....

ii. ....

iii. ....

2 Another way to add impact is to use **adjectives** to describe your nouns and **adverbs** to describe your verbs. For example:

> I saw giant seagulls flying down on to the golden sand as I walked slowly along the deserted beach.

a Choose the best of your sentences from question 1 b above and add 🖉 adjectives to your nouns and adverbs to one of the verbs.

i. .... ☐

....

ii. .... ☐

....

iii. .... ☐

....

b Which of your sentences is the most effective? Tick ✓ your choice. Write a sentence to explain why it is effective.

....

....

....

2 How do I use language techniques to create images?

You can add impact to your imaginative writing by using language techniques such as similes, metaphors and personification. These techniques will create powerful images in the minds of your readers.

1 Look at these examples of sentences that use language techniques.

A. The sea was like a glistening jewel.	Personification
B. The beach was a scorching furnace by midday.	Simile
C. The waves crept closer and closer to my feet.	Metaphor

a Draw lines 🖉 linking the sentences with the correct techniques.

b Choose one of the examples above and explain 🖉 what image it would create in a reader's mind.

....

....

....

....

2 Now use the techniques above to complete 🖉 these sentences.

Similes:

i. The sand looked like ....

....

ii. The seagulls swooped down like a ....

....

Metaphors:

i. The beach was ....

....

ii. The ice cream was ....

....

Personification (add verbs):

i. The wind .... against my face.

ii. Seaweed .... to my feet.

3 Write a short description of the beach using two of your ideas from question 2 .

....

....

....

....

....

3 How do I review and improve my vocabulary choices?

When you have finished your imaginative writing, you should always review your vocabulary choices.

1 First, look at your writing to see if it lacks impact. For instance, this student has made some boring vocabulary choices.

> We sat very close together on the warm bus. The sun in my eyes made me feel faint. I could smell my friend's crisps and hear him chewing loudly. Out of the window I could see green fields and lots of trees.

a Which words could be improved by substituting a more exciting synonym? Underline (A) them and note down (✐) alternatives for **two** of these words.

....

....

b Draw (✐) arrows where you could add adjectives and adverbs to the student's writing. Annotate the writing with **two** more adjectives and **one** adverb.

c Where could impact be added by using a language technique? Think of a simile, metaphor or an example of personification that would improve the writing and write (✐) it below.

....

....

2 Second, review your vocabulary to see if you have chosen words or phrases that are not very original. For instance, this student uses phrases that are so overused that they lack impact.

> Stella burst into floods of tears. She was normally as brave as a lion but something had really spooked her this time. I could see she was already frightened to death as she was white as a sheet.

a Underline (A) any words or phrases that you think are not very original.

b Select **one** and replace (✐) it with vocabulary or a language technique that is original enough to create impact.

....

....

....

c Now rewrite (✐) the paragraph, replacing the words and phrases you underlined in (a) with vocabulary that creates impact.

....

....

....

....

Sample response

When you select vocabulary for your imaginative writing, you should think about:

- using exciting verbs
- adding adjectives and adverbs to your nouns and verbs
- using similes, metaphors or personification to create powerful images
- reviewing all your vocabulary choices to make sure they are original and exciting.

Now look at one student's response to the beach picture you saw on page 65.

> I stared up at the shops and cafés that lined the beach. A cool summer breeze wafted over my face. As I strolled slowly along the fine golden sand the delicious smell of hotdogs floated towards me. Seagulls swooped onto the beach like vultures, pouncing on empty crisps packets and sandwich crusts.
>
> People trudged past me like an army going to war. When they reached the beach they set out their towels like carpets as their children rushed about clutching bright red buckets and spades. The waves lapped at their feet as they danced about in the water.

1. Underline (A) and label (✏) any examples of simile, metaphor and personification.
2. Circle (Ⓐ) **five** vocabulary choices that you feel add impact to the writing.
3. Choose **two** of the choices you have circled and explain (✏) the effect of the vocabulary.

....

....

4. For each of the highlighted words or phrases, think of **two** alternatives, then tick (✓) the ones you feel are most effective:

strolled slowly	.... ☐	.... ☐
fine golden	.... ☐	.... ☐
trudged	.... ☐	.... ☐
bright red	.... ☐	.... ☐
danced	.... ☐	.... ☐

Your turn!

You are now going to write your response to one of these exam-style tasks.

Exam-style question

Look at the images provided.

Write about a time when you, or someone you know, went on a day trip.

Your response can be real or imagined.

You may wish to base your response on one of the images. **(40 marks)**

(**1**) Think about all the different ideas you might include in your response. Use this space to note ✏ them down.

(**2**) Choose the ideas that you will focus on. Number ✏ them to show the structure you will use. Make sure you have added ✏ detail to each of your ideas.

(**3**) Now write ✏ your response on paper. Remember to focus on:

- using emotive language
- using language techniques to add impact.

(**4**) When you have finished writing, go back and review all your vocabulary choices. Amend ✏ any you think could be improved.

Review your skills

Check up

Review your response to the exam-style task on page 71. Tick ⊘ the column to show how well you think you have done each of the following.

	Not quite ⊘	Nearly there ⊘	Got it! ⊘
chosen words for effect	☐	☐	☐
used language techniques to create images	☐	☐	☐
reviewed and improved my vocabulary choices	☐	☐	☐

Look over all of your work in this unit. Note down ✎ **three** ways you can add impact through your vocabulary choices:

1. ....

2. ....

3. ....

Need more practice?

Tackle the exam-style question below.

Exam-style question

Look at the images provided. Write about a deserted town.

Your response can be real or imagined.
You may wish to base your response on one of the images.

(40 marks)

How confident do you feel about each of these **skills?** Colour ✎ in the bars.

1 How do I choose words for effect?
☐☐☐☐

2 How do I use language techniques to create images?
☐☐☐☐

3 How do I review and improve my vocabulary choices?
☐☐☐☐

Answers

Unit 1

Page 2

(1) Plan C: too many events mean nothing will be developed with interesting details

Plan B: no real ending to story

Plan A: story is dull and a bit predictable: no excitement for reader

Page 5

(1) For example:

Beginning: All my friends were jealous.

Middle: Have big breakfast and drive to race.

(3) **(a)** For example: Narrator could be hero as he could save best friend rather than winning.

(b) For example: Best friend could be villain as he could crash into narrator deliberately.

Unit 2

Page 10

(1) For example: Can be good for information/news; Good for comparing insurance and fuel bills; Good for planning holidays – all unsuitable for young audience.

(2) For example: Never speak online to strangers; Never save passwords online.

(3) For example: Easy to spend too long on games; Too much checking of social media is harmful

Page 11

(1) Write an <u>article</u> for a <u>national newspaper</u> about the <u>benefits of modern technology for older people.</u>

In your article, you could include:

- what <u>types of technology</u> are available
- <u>how</u> technology could make their <u>lives easier</u>
- <u>where</u> to get <u>help</u> with modern technology

(2) For example: writing – formal as newspaper readers not known personally; purpose – to inform about/ emphasise benefits and advise about technical aspects; audience – older readers of national newspaper; need to be reassured as might be apprehensive about using modern technology.

Page 13

(1) All TV channels are available on tablets. – 3

You can get apps on tablets to check your fuel bills. – 1

Tablets are cheaper than phones. – 2

(2) **(a)** Bullet 1 or 3 would be suitable.

(b) Bullet 2 is unsuitable.

Page 14

(1) **(a)** For example:

w: phones, tablets

h: useful apps, phones emergencies, online shopping, savings online, find old friends

wh: library, shop

(b) For example, music on phone

Unit 3

Page 19

(1) For example:

The lucky ending: The boy suggests they go for coffee; over coffee they both admit they pretended to be good skiers to impress each other.

Page 20

(1) A

Unit 4

Page 27

(1) **(a)** Points 1 and 4 are arguably the strongest.

Page 28

(1) Review – 75% of reality TV…; Letter – Not all reality TV…; Speech – Have you ever thought…?

(3) A

Page 29

(1) **(a)** question

(b) warning

Page 30

(1) and **(2)** For example: The introduction is dull and does not add enough detail to support the view of the writer. A technique such as a rhetorical question could be used, or a strong statistic to shock the audience.

Unit 5

Page 34

(1) **(a)** Both sentences are too long.

(b) Too many commas have been used instead of starting a new sentence.

(2) For example:

(a) Proper noun 'Barry' needs capital letter.

(b) Exclamation marks are overused.

(c) Apostrophe is missing from 'Barry's' and wrongly included in 'sells'.

(d) Sentences 4 and 5 could be joined as they are both about Barry's work in the restaurant.

Page 35

(1) For example: I loved my job in the **city. I** worked in a large fashion store and loved meeting lots of different people. I should never have moved to the country **as** I had to leave all my friends behind. The countryside was very green and peaceful **but** it was sometimes too quiet.

(2) For example: I only found out they were bulls when one charged at me!

③ For example: I always want to win even if I am just playing Monopoly with my mates! Who doesn't want to win? Those who say winning doesn't matter are just losers. They probably just don't want to try hard at anything. Competition is good for you as you learn something even if you don't come first.

Page 36

① ⓐ For example: Taking part in competitions is good for you but not everybody thinks winning is important.

ⓑ For example: We all need to learn what it is like to lose if we want to appreciate the joy of winning.

Page 37

① ⓐ For example: The weather was cold, blustery and very wet.

ⓑ For example: We all need to learn how to play fairly, how to lose gracefully and how to enjoy the game.

② ⓐ For example: My friend, who is very good at football, told me I was making a big mistake.

ⓑ For example: It was at the park, where I play netball every weekend, that I made my first mistake.

ⓒ For example: My first football trophy, which is silver-plated, stands on the mantelpiece.

Page 38

① For example:

My big mistake was telling everything to my friend Alice. Alice, the girl who lived next door, was the perfect friend and we did everything together. I thought she was the kindest, funniest person I had ever met. As we grew up, we shared clothes, make-up and even our deepest secrets about everything. When I met John, who was my brother's friend, at tennis lessons, I told Alice how much I liked him. I knew she would want to meet him. I didn't think that she would want him for herself!

Unit 6

Page 42

① A and B

② C

Page 43

① Sentences should use a variety of different openings.

Page 44

① For example: If we all stopped donating to charity, the government would have to do more about poverty.

② For example: I took my eyes off the road and turned to stare at her when I finally realised what she was telling me.

Page 46

For example:

① ⓐ There is some variety as the student has used an -ing verb, a preposition, an article and pronouns. This makes the paragraph more exciting to read.

ⓑ The sentence structures are varied.

ⓒ The final short sentence makes the reader want to know if anybody is hurt in the crash and what happens next. An alternative could be: 'I don't remember what happened next.'

Unit 7

Page 50

② Mark new paragraph before 'Most teenagers do not take the recommended amount of exercise

③ ⓐ teenagers spend lots of time in front of a computer screen

ⓑ most teenagers do not get enough exercise

④ Many teenagers, particularly boys, spend hours in front of computer games.

Girls spend hours on the internet.

I see young people catch the bus to school even if they live close enough to walk.

Page 51

① For example: Teenagers do not take enough daily exercise.

② For example:

i. Later, Ben remembered that day as the last time he was happy.

ii. Tom shut the back door firmly and walked into the lounge.

Page 52

① **Point:** Teenage obesity is a big problem in the UK. **Evidence:** A recent survey showed that eighty-five percent of teenagers do not take the recommended daily amount of exercise. Instead of playing sports outside, they are spending all their time in front of a computer screen. **Explanation:** This inactivity will make the obesity situation a lot worse if we do nothing.

② ⓐ/ⓑ For example: **Point:** Daily exercise has many benefits. **Evidence:** For example, it helps boost blood to your brain cells. **Explanation:** This means that even a short walk to school can help you get better grades in your GCSEs.

③ For example: Daily exercise has many benefits. I played football every lunchtime at school for the whole of Year 11. By the end of the year, I felt much fitter and had lost over a stone in weight.

Page 53

① For example:

5 He froze.

1 Ben's heart banged in his chest as he heard a sudden knocking at the door.

4 Standing in front of him was a man who was supposed to be dead.

2 His palms were sweaty and his breathing came in gasps.

3 Slowly he opened the door and peered out.

② He froze.

③ **a** For example: The doorbell rang just as Ben sat down. It had been a long and tiring day. All Ben could think about was his aching back, his sore feet and his frozen hands. Slowly getting to his feet, Ben shuffled towards the door. He opened it wide and looked out into the dark night. On the doorstep was a large black box.

b It was ticking.

Page 54

① For example:

a A new paragraph is needed because the action moves to the hall.

b The tense part is delayed until the end of the paragraph.

c The reader will want to know what happens in those five days.

Unit 8

Page 58

① them, their, they

② tiny, under-sized, inadequate

③ For example: Consequently, the animals just sit in there…

Furthermore, when someone walks past…

④ The rhetorical question adds impact by suddenly shifting the focus from the animals' plight to the humans who cause it, demanding that the reader take some blame for the situation.

Page 59

① **b** Version 2 is the more effective as it does not repeat the word 'animals'.

Page 60

①

Adding an idea:	Explaining an idea:	Introducing an example:
in addition additionally furthermore	as a result because therefore	for instance
Comparing or contrasting ideas:	Emphasising important ideas:	Ordering ideas:
likewise however on the other hand in contrast	significantly especially in particular	secondly next firstly in conclusion

② **a** For example – second paragraph:

<u>Firstly</u>, the animals used for testing are kept in appalling conditions. <u>For instance</u>, they are kept alone in tiny cages for most of the day with no light. They are taken out only when they are needed for experiments, all of which are very cruel. <u>Additionally</u>, they are even kept short of water and fed only enough to keep them alive. <u>As a result</u>, many start to pull out their own feathers or fur.

Page 61

① A – rhetorical question; B – list; C – direct address; D – repetition

Unit 9

Page 66

① **②** and **③** Student A's response contains effective descriptive vocabulary such as 'glistened', 'beautiful', 'lapped', 'scratchy', 'emerald', etc.

Page 68

① **a** A. – simile; B. – Metaphor; C. – personification

Published by Pearson Education Limited, 80 Strand, London, WC2R ORL.

www.pearsonschoolsandfecolleges.co.uk

Text © Pearson Education Limited 2017
Produced and typeset by Tech-Set Ltd, Gateshead

The right of Julie Hughes to be identified as author of this work has been asserted by her in accordance with the Copyright, Designs and Patents Act 1988.

First published 2017

20 19 18 17
10 9 8 7 6 5 4 3 2 1

British Library Cataloguing in Publication Data
A catalogue record for this book is available from the British Library

ISBN 978 0435 18328 8

Copyright notice
All rights reserved. No part of this publication may be reproduced in any form or by any means (including photocopying or storing it in any medium by electronic means and whether or not transiently or incidentally to some other use of this publication) without the written permission of the copyright owner, except in accordance with the provisions of the Copyright, Designs and Patents Act 1988 or under the terms of a licence issued by the Copyright Licensing Agency, Barnards Inn, 86 Fetter Lane, London EC4A 1EN(www.cla.co.uk). Applications for the copyright owner's written permission should be addressed to the publisher.

Printed in Slovakia by Neografia

Picture Credits
The publisher would like to thank the following for their kind permission to reproduce their photographs:

(Key: b-bottom; c-centre; l-left; r-right; t-top)

123RF.com: 1l, 6l, william87 65l, 66, 71l; **Shutterstock.com:** Dan Breckwoldt 65r, 71r, Dmitrijs Bindemanis 72l, Pressmaster 1r, 6r, Steven Castro 72r

All other images © Pearson Education